Flat Rock, Ohio 1910-1916

28 A

LITTLE
WOODS

CH
E

28 A

COW
FLOO
LOU

POND

SMOKE
HOUSE

23 A

WATER:
MELON
PATCH

WOOD
SHED

PLAY
YARD

ICE
HOUSE
WOOD
SHED

POULT
HOUS

13 A

GIRLS'
HOUSE

CONNECT
HALL
WAY

MAIN
BLDG
★

FOOT
PATH

HIRED
HELP

VEGYARD

FRONT YARD
FULL OF
TREES

HIRED
HELP

CHURCH

| | | | | | | | | | | | | | | | | | | | | / RAILROAD |

★ MAIN
3RD FLOOR
BOYS' BEDROOM
2ND FLOOR
HOSPITAL ROOMS
SCHOOL ROOMS
1ST FLOOR - IN WE ROOMS
LITTLE KIDS BEDRM

2 ACRES

The Orphan HOME

Flat Rock, Ohio 1910-1916

The Memories
of Laurence K.
John H. Buchholz

Edited by
Christine E. Buchholz Buck & John A. Buchholz

ORANGE FRAZER PRESS
Wilmington, Ohio

ISBN 1-933197-07-2
Copyright 2006 John A. Buchholz
First Orange Frazer Books Edition, 2006
Published by arrangement with Clear Spring Publishing

Additional copies of *THE ORPHAN HOME, FLAT ROCK, OHIO: 1910–1916: The Memories of Laurence K. and John H. Buchholz* may be ordered directly from:

Orange Frazer Press   or   Clear Spring Publishing
P.O. Box 214   P.O. Box 91
Wilmington, OH 45177   Greene, NY 13778

Telephone 1.800.852.9332 for   Telephone 1.607.656.5848 for
price and shipping information.   price and shipping information.
Website: www.orangefrazer.com   Website: www.clearspringpublishing.com

Layout & page design: Tim Fauley
Jacket design: Jeff Fulwiler

Library of Congress Cataloging-in-Publication Data

Buchholz, Laurence K., 1901–1992.
    The orphan home, Flat Rock, Ohio, 1910–1916 : the memories of Laurence K. and John H. Buchholz / edited by Christine E. Buchholz Buck & John A. Buchholz.-- 1st Orange Frazer Books ed.
        p. cm.
    ISBN 1-933197-07-2
    1. Ebenezer Orphan Home (Flat Rock, Ohio) 2. Buchholz, Laurence K., 1901-1992. 3. Buchholz, John H., d. 1994. 4. Orphans--Ohio--Flat Rock--Biography. 5. Orphanages--Ohio--Flat Rock. I. Buchholz, John H., d. 1994. II. Buck, Christine E. Buchholz, 1946- III. Buchholz, John A., 1936- IV. Title.

HV995.F52E243 2006
362.73'2--dc22
[B]

2005052320

For all Ebenezer orphans.

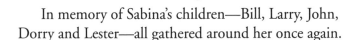

I hear of your kindness wherever my children are scattered. Oh, my sister won't I be the thankful mother when I can gather my little ones around me again. They are the greatest pleasure I ever had.

— Sabina Schroeder Buchholz, from a letter dated December 15, 1910, fifty-nine days before her death.

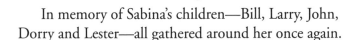

In memory of Sabina's children—Bill, Larry, John, Dorry and Lester—all gathered around her once again.

Sabina D., Willam E. and William C. Buchholz, c. 1900.
(Buchholz family archive)

$\mathcal{M}$ANY THANKS TO THE REV. CARL L. GRAY of the Flat Rock Home, who supplied document copies; Friedel Sonnenberg of the German Society of Pennsylvania, who helped to demystify inscrutable German longhand; and Ilerda Eckert Sauerwine, an Ebenezer orphan who provided the 1912 postcard that is this book's cover. It was verboten for her to taste the butter she churned in the milk cellar, so she spread stolen lard on stolen bread and imagined.

Special thanks to Orange Frazer's John Baskin for his early encouragement and Marcy Hawley for her patient, sage counsel.

The audiotapes from which this book grew were recorded between 1980 and 1983 by Christine E. Buchholz Buck and Melanie C. Buchholz Shaffner. They were transcribed by Christine Buck, who also translated related documents written in German. Tapes recorded and transcribed between 1990 and 1994 by John A. Buchholz provided additional material, as did *Memories*, a comprehensive autobiography written in 1993 and 1994 by John H. Buchholz.

$\mathcal{I}$N SEPTEMBER, 1910, WITH SHIPPING TAGS TIED to their clothing, John and Laurence Buchholz—six and eight—were put aboard a Lehigh Valley passenger train in Geneva, New York, for the first leg of their 360-mile journey to a rural Ohio orphanage.

This account of childhood at the Ebenezer Orphan Home in Flat Rock, Ohio, was drawn from conversations recorded during their later years.

The Orphan HOME

Flat Rock, Ohio   1910-1916

220	
1035	Buckholz Lawrence K. Buchholz was born at Geneva, N. Y. Nv. 23, 1901 and came to the Home Sept. 12, 1910 Father living W. C. Buchholz, mother died soon after boy came to the Home.
1036	Buckholz John Herbert Buchholz, was born at Geneva, N. Y. Sept. 15, 1903 and came to the Home with his brother as above.

1911 Orphan Home Journal Entry
(Flat Rock Home archive)

A SHORT TIME BEFORE THE BIRTH OF HER LAST CHILD—

a son—in September, 1908, Sabina Buchholz, 33, of 281 Washington Street, Geneva, New York, learned that she had tuberculosis.

As her condition deteriorated, she was compelled to leave her husband, William, and five children for sanitarium care. Mounting medical bills, domestic expenses and the resulting loss of his business eventually forced William to mortgage their home for nearly its full value.

Ultimately, the house was lost, and the burden of caring for the children and holding the young family together became impossible.

By 1910, relatives were providing interim care for the children. Later that year, satisfactory long-term arrangements appeared likely for William, the eldest; Doris, the only girl; and Lester, the youngest, not yet two.

Homes were not found for Laurence, eight, and John, six.

(Translated from German)

Geneva, New York
August 8, 1910
Rev. William H. Messerschmidt
Orphanfather
Ebenezer Orphan Home
Flat Rock, Ohio

Dear Brother Messerschmidt:

The Lord be with you!

I see myself led to write to you as Orphanfather of our church about a situation with which I am familiar.

Brother H. C. Schroeder is a strong, loyal, upright member of our church here. His daughter, Sabina Buchholz, has been ill for two years and has been unable for this whole time to take care of her family and household. This week, she will again be taken to a sanitarium, where she must certainly remain for several months. It is doubtful if she can be helped.

Now, genuine need and the sad situation of the children have caused me, after long hesitation, to contact you.

The five children—four boys about twelve, eight, six and one and one-half years, and a girl about four years old—have been taken care of by strangers, and partially by Father and Mother Schroeder. The Schroeders are not wealthy people, and Mother Schroeder is in somewhat poor health, so they are able to provide continuing care for but one of the children.

The parents of the children are members of our church, and, in addition to the sad plight of the mother, are now penniless and very much to be pitied. And the good children even more so. These children are not orphans—not as yet—but even so, they are worthy of the compassion of the church.

Request: Could not the two boys, eight and six years old, find shelter in our home in view of this persistent and grievous situation?

Dear Brother, even if it might be only for a temporary period, let me know one way or the other as soon as possible.

I send a thousand hearty greetings.
Your Brother,
Geo. Ott, Preacher in Charge
Evangelical Association, Geneva, N. Y.

In the autumn of 1910, with shipping tags attached to their clothing, Larry and John Buchholz were taken to the Lehigh Valley station in Geneva and put aboard a passenger train to Buffalo. There, they were transferred to the Nickel Plate line bound for Bellevue, Ohio, near their ultimate destination: The Ebenezer Orphan Home in Flat Rock, 360 miles from home.

APPLICATION

FOR THE ADMISSION OF *John H. Buchholz* ~~AN ORPHAN,~~ INTO

THE EBENEZER ORPHAN HOME

OF THE EVANGELICAL ASSOCIATION. *No 1036*

FLAT ROCK, SENECA CO. OHIO.
p. 220

Name of child in full: *John Herbert Buchholz*

Place and date of birth of child: *Geneva N.Y. Sept 15. 1903.*

Full name of father: *William Charles Buchholz*

Place and date of his Birth: *Geneva N.Y. March 22d 1874.*

Full (and maiden) name of mother: *Sabina D. nee Schroeder*

Place and date of her birth: *Waterloo N.Y. June 25th 1875.*

When and where did father die?: ....

When and where did mother die?: *Died soon after child came — Sept*

Cause of death: ....

Church relation, if any, of father: *Member of the Evangelical Association, Geneva, N.Y.*

 "   "   "   "   mother: *the same*

Number and age of brothers: *Three, besides self 12 + 9. 2. Years old.*

 "   "   "   "   sisters: *One sister 5. Years old.*

Is the child really a poor orphan?: *Yes.*

What are the financial circumstances of parent? State fully on back: *they are not good. Common circumstances*

What are h..... grade and standing at school?: *2 grade standing 95. Deportment 98.*

Has the child any bad habits?: *Not any.*

What are they?: ....

What is the moral standing and character of the child?: *Very good:*

Remarks: ....

Dated *Geneva, N.Y.* Sign (parent or guardian) *W. C. Buchholz.*
August 13th 19*10.*

PHYSICIAN'S CERTIFICATE.

Have you thoroughly examined (name of child) *John Herbert Buchholz*

Is ...he in perfect health?: *Yes.*

Is ...he of sound mind?: *Yes.* Has ...he perfect vision?: *Yes.*

Is ...he free from any cutaneous or other contagious disease?: *Yes.*

Has ...he suffered from or been exposed to any such disease recently?*: *No*

Is ...he subject to epileptic or other fits?: *No.* To regular or frequent wetting the bed?: *No.*

Remarks: ....

Dated *Geneva N.Y. August 20. 1910.* Sign *William N. Hoskin* M.D.

---

* N. B.- No child should be sent to this Home who has been recently exposed to Smallpox, Measles, Whooping Cough, Dyphtheria, or any contagious disease whatever. The risk is too great.

(Flat Rock Home archive)

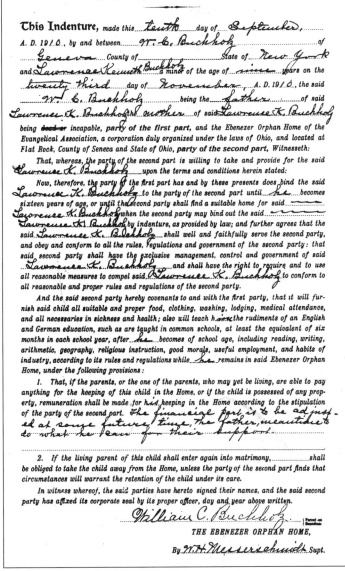

CONTRACT.

This Indenture, made this *tenth* day of *September,* A. D. 19*10*, by and between *W. C. Buchholz* of *Geneva* County of State of *New York* and *Lawrence Kenneth Buchholz* a minor of the age of *nine* years on the *twenty third* day of *November,* A. D. 19*10*, the said *W. C. Buchholz* being the *father* of said *Lawrence K. Buchholz* the *mother* of said *Lawrence K. Buchholz* being ~~dead or~~ incapable, party of the first part, and the Ebenezer Orphan Home of the Evangelical Association, a corporation duly organized under the laws of Ohio, and located at Flat Rock, County of Seneca and State of Ohio, party of the second part, Witnesseth:

That, whereas, the party of the second part is willing to take and provide for the said *Lawrence K. Buchholz* upon the terms and conditions herein stated:

Now, therefore, the party of the first part has and by these presents does bind the said *Lawrence K. Buchholz* to the party of the second part until *he* becomes sixteen years of age, or until the second party shall find a suitable home for said *Lawrence K. Buchholz* when the second party may bind out the said *Lawrence K. Buchholz* by indenture, as provided by law; and further agrees that the said *Lawrence K. Buchholz* shall well and faithfully serve the second party, and obey and conform to all the rules, regulations and government of the second party: that said, second party shall have the exclusive management, control and government of said *Lawrence K. Buchholz* and shall have the right to require and to use all reasonable measures to compel said *Lawrence K. Buchholz* to conform to all reasonable and proper rules and regulations of the second party.

And the said second party hereby covenants to and with the first party, that it will furnish said child all suitable and proper food, clothing, washing, lodging, medical attendance, and all necessaries in sickness and health; also will teach *him* the rudiments of an English and German education, such as are taught in common schools, at least the equivalent of six months in each school year, after *he* becomes of school age, including reading, writing, arithmetic, geography, religious instruction, good morals, useful employment, and habits of industry, according to its rules and regulations while *he* remains in said Ebenezer Orphan Home, under the following provisions:

1. That, if the parents, or the one of the parents, who may yet be living, are able to pay anything for the keeping of this child in the Home, or if the child is possessed of any property, remuneration shall be made for *his* keeping in the Home according to the stipulation of the party of the second part. *The financial part is to be adjusted at some future time, the father, meantime to do what he can for their support.*

2. If the living parent of this child shall enter again into matrimony, shall be obliged to take the child away from the Home, unless the party of the second part finds that circumstances will warrant the retention of the child under its care.

In witness whereof, the said parties have hereto signed their names, and the said second party has affixed its corporate seal by its proper officer, day and year above written.

William C. Buchholz | Parent or Guardian

THE EBENEZER ORPHAN HOME,

By *W. H. Messerschmidt* Supt.

(Flat Rock Home archive)

(Larry)

It was September of 1910 when we left to go out there. We went all the way by ourselves. No one took us there. I was eight and John was six.

(John)

And it's strange that I don't remember going to the depot in Geneva, or who took us there. But I do recall waiting for the train. Larry remembers it better than I do.

I remember that before we got on the train, they tied shipping tags on us. Right on our shirt buttons.

Pop told the conductor, "Now you take these fellows to the station in Buffalo and transfer them to the Nickel Plate. Tell that conductor to take care of them and put them off in Bellevue, Ohio."

And that's what happened. When we got to Buffalo, the conductor took us over to the Nickel Plate, and he told the conductor there, "Now these boys are going to Flat Rock, Ohio. To an orphan home. It's up to you to take care of them. See that you do it."

Then John and I got on that train. It was a long way out there. It seemed like an eternal ride.

We finally pulled into the station in Bellevue at two the

following morning. I remember that it was raining, it was cold, and the wind was blowing. Father Messerschmidt, the superintendent of the orphanage, was there to meet us.

He was a giant of a man with gray hair and a big, bushy beard.

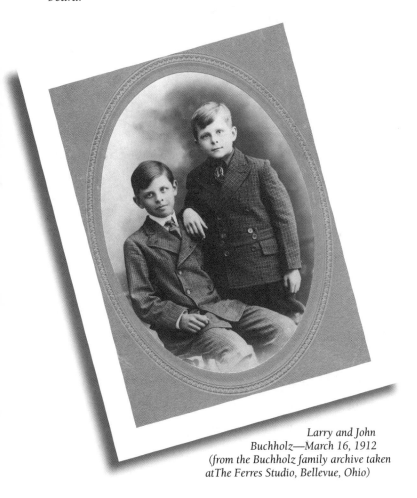

*Larry and John
Buchholz—March 16, 1912
(from the Buchholz family archive taken
at The Ferres Studio, Bellevue, Ohio)*

He was pulled up to the station in a surrey with side curtains on it. He was standing there when we got off the train. I don't remember what he said, but he took us right over to the surrey and drove us out to the Home, about three miles away.

There was a long driveway going in, with pine trees on each side. The wind was howling and whistling through those trees, and I can remember seeing lights in the big building, way in the back. It looked like a penitentiary. I tell you, if I ever felt homesick, that was the time.

Father Messerschmidt took us into the main building, and Julius Zimmerman—a moron—was waiting there to take our luggage. We learned later that he was somehow related to Mother Messerschmidt, and was called "Mikie Dobber" by all the kids.

He was simple-minded.

He scared me. He had a big nose and heavy lips. And he slobbered a lot.

He had trouble with his bladder, too. He had a tube coming down his leg, and whenever he had to go, he'd just unscrew that thing and go someplace.

He took us up to the big bedroom on the third floor and put us to bed.

And it seemed like John and I had just fallen asleep when, "Clang! Clang! Clang!" a matron—Old Lady Wetzel, they called her—was standing there ringing a bell and turning on all the lights, getting all the kids up.

It was four-thirty in the morning.

She said, "You two boys can stay in bed a little while longer, because you're new and you went to bed late." That was the first and last kind thing that she ever did for us.

As little as I had seen of Larry before, I saw less of him after we got there, because they immediately split us up. I was put in the little boys' sitting room and bedroom, and he was put in the big boys' area. Even the yards where we played, out back of the main building, were fenced and I had to stay on my side and Larry on his.

Whenever we could, when he was in his yard and I was in mine, we'd go down toward the end of the fence where we could be alone. It was like being in jail, really. Sometimes, when we were homesick, we'd hold hands through the fence.

We had to mingle in with the rest of the children right away. Imagine—forty or fifty of them that we didn't even know. I had never had contact with that many kids before.

It was difficult making acquaintances with the other boys. There was an established pecking order, and you had to make your own way into it by licking a couple of them before you had any standing.

I had never fought anyone before. Back home, some guy would come up to me and stick his finger in my face and I'd say, "I give up! I give up!" There was no sense in fighting. But at the Orphan Home, you had no choice. You were forced to establish your position.

I remember one morning, after I had been there a little while, Gus Kraft and Bill Beck—two big guys—came up to me and said, "After breakfast, you're going to fight somebody."

I was scared. I tried to get away from them. I didn't want to fight anybody. After breakfast, I ran out of the dining room and beat it into the mop closet under the back stairs and crawled underneath the bottom step. I pulled all the buckets and stuff in there around me. But they found me.

The first kid I had to fight was Babe Clymer, Nig's brother. I didn't want to fight him, but he hit me and it started. I just stood there and whaled away. Bare fists. I had to fight five guys, one right after the other. I had a bloody nose and I was all black and blue, but I established myself out there. I moved up the line—the chairs that went around the perimeter of the big boys' sitting room. Your chair signified your rank.

Later, I wanted to move up a few more pegs. Stricker was maybe two or three chairs ahead of me, so I challenged him to a fight. I said, "Well, Stricker, let's go out behind the barn," and we went out to the old barn and argued for a while about who could lick who, you know.

Then we fought until we could hardly stand up. I tell you, our own mothers wouldn't have recognized us. My arms hurt and my face was all beaten out of shape—really swollen up. Neither of us won, but he had a lot of respect for me after that.

One thing about the Orphan Home: you weren't out there very long before you knew the regimen. When somebody said, "Don't," you didn't, or you were punished with a vengeance. It didn't take long to learn. When they were going to give you a licking, you had to go into Father Messerschmidt's office—the main office.

You had to take down your pants and lie over a chair. Then they would take harness straps, tongue straps or lacing to you. Father Messerschmidt was a kindly old patriarch. He'd only give you three or four good whacks. But Mother Messerschmidt was usually the one that did it. She tried to make you cry.

Everybody tried not to, though, because crying denoted weakness and they didn't want to give her any satisfaction.

But some of them cried. It was hard not to.

How many kids do we remember? Well, if we heard their names, we could remember what most of them looked like. I could, anyway. Fred Bailey and John Schrader...

...Lawrence Schrader, Lawrence Smith, Robert Smith, John Hershey, and Skunk Perry.

We called him Skunk because he wet the bed. But Miss Frank said, "You shouldn't call him Skunk, because that isn't very nice." So after that we called him American Skunk, and that took care of it as far as we were concerned.

The matron took some of us on a shopping trip to Bellevue once. We went to the five and dime store, and some of the kids picked up little toys and things, so I picked out something that I wanted and started to walk out the door with it. The matron, or maybe the store clerk—I don't remember which—said, "You can't have that. You didn't pay for it." I didn't have any money, and I didn't understand that I had to have it. Nobody ever told me. So I had to put it back. I was embarrassed and felt very badly about it.

I remember getting a letter from my mother a short time after we were sent to the Home. She said that she hoped we liked it there and were making lots of friends. She said that she loved us and hoped that we could come home to her soon.

One day that winter, in 1911, about five months after we got there, they called me down out of the schoolroom on the second floor and told me that Mrs. Wetzel wanted to see me in the living room. I thought maybe I was going to get a licking. I went into the living room, and she was standing there, and I walked up to her, and she said, "Your Mother is dead," and turned around and walked away. Just like that.

You told me that Mom had died. We couldn't go back home for her funeral. We were quarantined because some of the children had scarlet fever. I don't know whether they would have allowed us to go if we hadn't been quarantined, but we were, so there wasn't any question about it.

Somebody from back home sent me Mother's obituary with a dried, pressed flower. At the bottom of the obituary it said, "Please omit flowers." I often wondered about that, because she loved flowers so much. Somebody did tell me later, though, that there was one wreath on her grave. I think that my pressed flower may have come from that wreath.

I don't remember getting any letters from home after my mother died, but a package came from my brother Bill one day. It was a "Magic Lantern"—an early slide projector.

It had a built-in oil lamp as a light source, so the pictures were pretty dim. Most of the slides were of outdoor scenery. It had a kaleidoscope attachment, and you could turn a crank and the colors and patterns would change. I used to project pictures onto a bed sheet in the cloak room, but one night Mother Messerschmidt caught some of us in there and made me stop because of the danger of fire.

We had to get up at four-thirty in the summertime and five in the winter to go out and do the chores that were assigned to us. From the day we got there, we had an obligation to perform certain jobs. I can remember that I had to mop the porch of the main building. I had to get out there every morning with a bucket of soap and water and mop it down. And that was one long porch!

We had to do specific jobs every day. My first job was

making beds in the little boys' room. There were at least twenty beds in there—cots really, not beds—and I had to make four of them every morning.

I remember in the spring of 1911, a few months after we got there, we had to take the mattresses off the beds in the little boys' room and put drops of kerosene between the boards where the real small interlocking springs fastened in. You should have seen the bedbugs crawl out!

Another job that I had to do for a while was scrub toilets and clean the outhouse—a six-holer.

A lot of fights took place behind that outhouse. Down at the end of the yard.

Later on, I graduated to mopping floors in the little boys' sitting room, and from there to carrying coal and wood from the shed into the kitchen for the cook stove.

There was a ramp going up to the second floor of the barn, and under it they had a fruit cellar where they stored potatoes. About the time we had to go out and sort, half of them were rotten. And if you've ever gotten ahold of a rotten potato, you'll know why that sticks in my mind.

I helped make apple butter, too. We used that as a substitute for real butter. I had to boil the cider down and stir it. It was all on schedule. You were assigned harder tasks as you got older.

The girls did the sewing and mending, and they helped with the cooking and cleaning. They washed all the bedding and clothes in a big rotary washing machine—a huge tub out in the power house—and they did all the ironing on two huge mangle machines. They baked all the bread in an oven in the power house, too. When it was done, they took it out of the oven with big wooden paddles.

Clara Diehl, Clara Christ, Ilerda Eckert, Ebenezer Orphan Home, Flat Rock, OH. c. 1912. (Eckert-Sauerwine family archive)

28

The kuchen! Remember? Great big holes in it, and brown sugar and raisins. That was a treat!

The girls cleaned their bedrooms and did the preserving and canning. They helped with the cooking, too. We all ate together in the big dining room in the main building, girls on one side and boys on the other. The girls who worked in the kitchen brought the food out to the tables. We ate family-style.

Do you remember the time one of the kids complained about the food they gave us for supper one night?

That was Babe Clymer. The cook came out of the kitchen and hauled him right up off the bench. She dragged him up to the front of the room and made him stand at one of the tables up there. Then she brought out a big bowl of awful-looking slop that she had made with tomatoes and all kinds of chopped-up stuff. It was edible, but it made you sick to look at it.

She said, "All right. You don't like the food? Try this and see how you like it!"

He refused to eat it, and he just stood there until supper was over. He went to bed hungry that night, and he never complained about the food again.

The first time I ever heard a player piano was in the dining room. A man who worked at the orphanage would come in once in a while and play it for us while we were having dinner. I remember one of the songs he used to play was "Star of the East." All that music—the keys moving up and down and nobody touching them! I thought that was a wonderful machine!

Every year, in the spring, they took our shoes from us. We had no shoes until fall, when it began to get cold. But all summer we had to go barefooted—working out in the fields pitching grain, shocking and stacking wheat, pitching hay, stacking oats and cutting corn—walking in the stubble. All of it barefooted.

And you'd step on those sharp corn spikes, you know, where you cut it off with the corn knife. Imagine nineteen or twenty barefooted little kids going down the cornfield, one in each row, with machetes, cutting corn. Then we'd have to take it over and stack it and tie it up in shocks. The corn leaves were sharp as all-get-out, and our necks and ears used to get all cut up.

I remember one morning Larry and I were playing out in the new barn. I don't know whether it was a holiday or not, but we weren't working, and we were barefooted. I stepped on a board that had a rusty nail in it, and I didn't do anything about it. Then in the afternoon we were out in the old barn and I stepped on a spike with the other foot. You could see it poking the skin up through the side.

I remember that both of your feet were tied up.

Didn't get lockjaw, either.

When Larry and I worked together in the barn, it was our chore to go get the cows on cold fall mornings. They were usually way down by the woods. It seemed like two miles at the time, but I don't believe it was actually more than a quarter of a mile away.

Down in the Thirty-one. When I say "Thirty-one," I'm talking about acres. Each field was known by its acreage.

One frosty morning we were still barefooted, and by the time we got all the way down there, our feet were almost frozen. The cows were over by the woods, lying under some trees. After we cleared them out, we ran over and stood where they had been sleeping to try to warm our feet. But by the time we got them started down the lane, our feet were freezing again. So we followed the cows, and whenever one of them flopped, we ran over and stood in it. It was nice and warm.

When we got back, there was a pipe outside the main building that had holes in it—a spray pipe. We turned that on and the water shot out, and we washed our feet.

I remember going home from the barn one time. I don't know how old I was, but I was only a little kid. I'd been doing some chores up there, and we had the wagon hooked up to two horses. One's name was Fred. You remember Fred?

No, I remember Ben.

I said to him, "I'm not going to walk all the way back there." So I got on his back.

That horse considered it an indignity for me to get on him after he'd been working all day. He didn't want me on his back no-how! He kicked and jumped, and the other one was right beside him, and he was scared and kicking too, and they headed for the new barn.

I was hanging on for dear life! But when they got to the water tank they stopped and I fell off and they started drinking. Man alive! I thought I was going to get killed! I was just a little kid!

Oh, when we discovered the swimming hole! It was fed by springs, but it was a mud hole. It was just the color of chocolate ice cream. And it was in the Seventeen where they used to put the cows, and the cows would wander out and get in the pond.

Kids used to go swimming in there. Took off all your clothes, and there'd be fifteen kids over there diving around in that dirty water.

And crabs!

We used to take a string and drop it down and a crab would grab ahold of it, and you'd jerk it out and get the crab and take his claws off.

We'd do crazy things. Terrible things. And remember down in Goode's Pond, the snakes that were in there? I don't know what kind of snakes they were. Just ordinary water snakes, maybe. But we used to sneak down there. That was down by the Eighty acres.

*The Girls'
Dormitory Building shortly
after its completion in 1912.*
(Flat Rock Home archive)

The girls' house was started in 1911 and finished in 1912. When they dug the foundation hole for that building, they needed stone in the bottom as a base for the concrete floor. And there were lots of stones in the yard and field next to it that they wanted to get rid of.

So Father Messerschmidt made a game of it. He put one stone on top of another at the edge of the hole and said to a bunch of us, "O.K., boys, see if you can knock that stone off there!" So we'd pick up rocks and throw them at it, and of course they'd go down in the hole, right where he wanted them. When he got enough in one area, he'd move the target, and eventually, we threw all the stones they needed down into that hole. And I'll bet every one of them is still there!

About the time that the girls' building was finished, Uncle Elmer and Aunt Lena—she was actually our half-aunt, our mother's half-sister—graduated from college and came to the orphan home to teach for a year before Uncle Elmer went to medical school.

We were happy when they got there. We thought we'd finally get some love and understanding. But you know, they never gave us a break at all.

As a matter of fact, it was worse for us after they got there.

They used us as examples.

They'd say, "Now see? This is my nephew. Don't you do what he just did, or here's what you're going to get!" They went out of their way to avoid showing any kindness toward us, and the net result was that they treated us worse than anyone else.

I was homesick one day, so I wrote a letter home to Pop and said, "Everybody's mean to us out here. Please take us out of here. We want to come home." Uncle Elmer saw me writing that letter.

In the living room, one wall had a tier of boxes, and each box was about ten by twelve inches. There were no lids on them, but they slid in and out, and each kid had his own box to put his things in. Nobody ever went into anybody else's box. It was a matter of honor.

I put my letter in there.

Uncle Elmer went in and took it out of my box and opened it and read it. After school he said, "You stay here."

He got part of a harness and took off his glasses and put them on his desk. Then he said, "Come over here." And he held my arm and beat me with that strap. I tried not to cry, but it was a terrible beating.

I went up to bed, but I couldn't lie on my back. I had to lie on my stomach.

I remember that night. You came in with your shirt off, and I don't think there was one spot on your back an inch wide that didn't have a welt at least the size of a quarter.

I'll never forget that. I don't know why I ever forgave him. I shouldn't have.

I was sitting at my desk in Aunt Lena's class one day, and I wanted to go over and sit with the kid next to me, like some of the others had done because there weren't enough books to go around. So, before class started, I tore the geography lesson for that day out of my book and stuck it in my pocket. Then I raised my hand and said, "I don't have today's lesson in my book."

Stupid.

Aunt Lena said, "Well, it was in there before class when I borrowed it to look something up. Why don't you have it now?"

Then she called me up front, got a wooden ruler and took my hand in hers. She raised the ruler and came down hard, but I yanked my hand away and she hit herself. She was hopping mad! She banged me over the head and knocked me all over the place!

They had to be strict to a degree, I suppose. Sometimes we deserved it.

There was a woods, oh, I imagine nearly a mile away from the Home. We used to call them the Pawpaw Woods. The kids used to go down there and get pawpaws.

Pawpaws grow on a tree and look almost like a pear.

We used to get them, and it sort of helped us along when we didn't get enough to eat.

Remember the thorn apples we used to eat too?

Yeah, we used to get those little thorn apples and eat them. And walnuts. When walnuts were ripe in the fall we used to go down to the woods and get them and take them up and shuck them. There was a tin roof out on the wagon shed. I don't think it was flat, but it was almost flat.

It had a slight angle.

Just a gentle slope on it. And we would put our walnuts up on that roof and dry them. And, by golly, one thing about it, nobody ever took anybody else's walnuts. They were sacred property.

Yes, sir. The same with our boxes in the living room.

Remember the first time we were up in the belfry on the main building? That was the tall, three-story building. The main building.

Oh, boy, I'll say so.

We had to sneak up there. I'll never forget that day. Was that on the Fourth of July?

Yeah. A holiday.

EBENEZER ORPHAN HOME
FLAT ROCK, OHIO.

School record of *Laurence Buchholz*

Fifth Grade, for the year beginning *Sept. 2,* 19 *12*.

	1st Mo.	2nd Mo.	3rd Mo.	4th Mo.	5th Mo.	6th Mo.	7th Mo.	8th Mo.	9th Mo.		Av
Reading	96	97	97	98	96	96	93	97	92	97	96	97
Writing	92	94	94	95	96	96	96	94	93	95	94	95
Spelling	98	98	99	99	100	98	99	95	99	94	98	96
Language	89	93	89	92	88	92	92	94	94	83	91	
Arithmetic	78	83	90	84	86	83	75	85	87	79	83	
Geography	94	93	97	92	94	96	90	96	93	99	94	
History	83	91	89	88	92	87	93	83	90	88	88	
Grammar												
Drawing												
Physiology	88	90	99	99	90	92	90	100	100	97	94	
German	95	95	95	95	96	89	91	90	93		94	94
Days Present	*Average 72*											
Times Tardy	*Promoted to sixth Grade*											
Habits												

Remarks:

Date *June 6,* 19 *13.* *Mrs. E. W. Schmalzried*

TEACHER.

(Buchholz family archive)

When everyone was out at lunch, we snuck in the front door and up those steps. When we got up there, we carved our initials up there. You remember?

Do you remember the pitch of the roof?

Sure I do.

Main Building, Ebenezer Orphan Home c. 1920.
(Flat Rock Home archive)

One day Father Messerschmidt asked for someone to go up and get something out of the eaves. Probably a ball. So I went up there. Do you remember how I got up in the belfry and then had to go out along the pitch of the roof? That roof was slate, no less.

While we were out there, Pop came out twice. The first time, I imagine, was in 1912. It was after Mother had died, I know. And when he got there, somebody said, "Your father's here," but I didn't recognize him. I don't know whether you did or not.

I recognized him.

We didn't have to work while he was there. I guess he was there for two days, wasn't he?

I believe he was there overnight, anyway. I think he came out one afternoon and went back the next. The day he got there, we all went down to the woods.

He brought Larry and me each a jackknife, and he took us down to the woods and carved our initials in a tree. Remember? When he left, I'll never forget that the three of us stood in the front yard and sang, "God Be With You Till We Meet Again."

I won't either. We sang it—John and I, and Pop.

And when he left, I had the deepest sense of desolation that I've ever had in my life. And to this day I can't sing "God Be With You" without having tears come.

We talked a lot about running away. We were tired of all the hard work and the beatings for every little infraction. We didn't know where we would go, but we thought that anyplace would be better than the Orphan Home.

We saved every crust of bread we could get our hands on and wrapped them up in anything we could find: sheets of paper, pages from the Sears Roebuck catalog. Then we took them over and buried them in the coal shed. When we saved enough, we decided we'd go.

It was dusk, and we got the bread and started down the lane. But when we got to the end, we had no idea which way to go, and it was close to the woods, you know, and dark and scary.

John said, "Don't you think we ought to wait until after supper?"

I said, "Yeah, maybe we'd better."

So we turned around and went back to the Home, and that was the end of that.

I'm still waiting for the nickel that Larry owes me.

You know, a nickel was a lot of money out there. If you had a nickel, you were rich. Pop sent us two dollars each while we were out there. That was all the money we had for six years.

But we didn't get it directly. It went to the office and they rationed it out to us. Every once in a while we were allowed to draw out a nickel or a dime. So one day we went into the office and withdrew a nickel each. I hung onto mine, but Larry spent his.

A few days later, I was in the little kids' yard and he was on his side of the fence. He called me over to where we could talk and said, "Do you still have your nickel?" I said, "Yeah." He said, "Let me have it." I said, "No. I'm not going to give it to you." So he said, "If you don't give it to me, I'm going to climb up that chimney over there and drop on that lightning rod and kill myself!"

So I gave him the nickel. And I never got it back.

I couldn't have climbed up on that lightning rod, anyway. That thing was four stories high.

During the summer, we had Sunday night suppers on the front lawn and a cookie or a little cake for dessert. When the kids didn't have money, they'd use those cookies and cakes as a medium of exchange. They'd bargain with other kids for something they wanted, and buy it on credit.

They'd pay one cookie or cake every Sunday until their debt was paid off. And everybody paid their cookies and cakes religiously. Maybe a little reluctantly, though.

One day a kid told me he'd give me a nickel if I'd sneak into Flat Rock—there was a little grocery store there, and maybe fifteen or sixteen houses—and buy him some red hot cinnamon drops. Of course, there was a strict rule against leaving the grounds. We weren't even allowed in the front yard, except on the Fourth of July and Sunday afternoons during the summer.

But a nickel was big money. Flat Rock was just down the road past the church, so I knew I wouldn't be gone very long. I figured that my chances of getting caught were pretty slim.

I made it into Flat Rock with no problem. It was a beautiful day and I was enjoying the walk back, carrying the red hots in a paper bag, when I saw a lady and a girl walking down the road toward me. As they got closer, I realized that it was Mother Messerschmidt and her daughter Caroline.

I didn't know what to do. There was no avenue of escape. There wasn't any corn field I could dive into, and it was too late to run anyplace.

I couldn't dream up any good reason for being out there on the road, so as I approached her, I tried to appear businesslike and I walked fast, you know, like I'd been sent on an errand by somebody. I said, "Good morning, Mother Messerschmidt," as I passed her.

But she said, "Just a minute!" and asked me where I'd been and what I had in the bag. I told her, and she said, "You go to the office and wait there for me."

I knew I was in for it. I went to the office and waited. Pretty soon, Father Messerschmidt walked in and asked me what I was doing there. So I told him the whole story, and that Mother Messerschmidt had sent me to the office to wait for her.

He said, "Stay here," and then he left. In a while, he came back. I was pretty scared. Then he said, "You know what you did was wrong. Don't do it again. You can go now."

While I was in the little kids' bedroom, I had the mumps and the measles, but not at the same time. Did you get them?

No. I had them before we got there. I remember when you had them, though.

You know, there must have been at least a hundred and fifty kids there—both girls and boys. And we had those epidemics of scarlet fever, whooping cough and measles, and all that other stuff. Yet, all the time we were there, not one kid died. And that, in itself, is remarkable.

Because the doctor was a veterinarian.

That's what he was. Doc Schumaker. He had his office in Flat Rock, and they'd call him whenever the cows got sick. And he used to come into the home at noontime with a box full of different kinds of candy to sell to the kids. And he did dental work, too.

He used one of those old treadle drills.

Boy! He got me one time! He was working on me and the drill broke off in my tooth. It was laying right on a nerve, and he couldn't get it out. I'll never forget that. I thought I was going to die! But he finally got it out.

Some of us dug a secret tunnel leading out of the fenced-in yard. We put boards and dirt and grass over it, and when Old Lady Wetzel wasn't watching, we'd crawl into the tunnel and under the fence and run out to the orchard to get apples. She watched us every chance she got, but she never knew we could escape from the back yard any time we wanted to. Nobody would ever tell her.

There was a big swing frame out in the play yard, but we never had any swings.

Some of the big kids told me once, "If you ever tell Old

Lady Wetzel anything, we'll nail you in a box, tie it up with ropes, pull it up over the swing, and throw rocks at it until it breaks open and you fall out.

Remember the cross some of the kids made? If anybody ever told on anybody else, they'd tie him up on it and throw stones at him. They did that! At a church orphanage! Our relatives back home never had any idea what kind of a place that was!

Everybody despised Old Lady Wetzel. She was a mean one. The kids all thought she looked like a big bird with skinny legs, so they made up a little rhyme that they used to chant behind her back.

"Over the hill, a great way off, the jaybird died of the whooping cough!"

She finally left the orphanage, and that certainly was one happy day. When we heard that she was gone, we all gathered out in the back yard. We had a big celebration and cheered, "Hooray, hooray, hooray, hooray! Old Lady Wetzel's gone away!"

Regina Frank took her place.

Dooty. What was Dooty's name?

I don't remember her first name, but everybody called her "Needlenose."

That's right. She had a pointed nose. Needlenose D-O-O-T-Y. She married the fellow who worked in the power house.

His name was Cooper. I had a big wart on my knuckle, and one day he asked me if I wanted him to take it off. I said I did, and he put the head of a kitchen match on it and lit it with another match. Burned it off. Hurt like hell for a few days, but it never came back.

Dooty was the first matron I had in the little boys' room. She was the one that I was afraid to tell when I stabbed myself with the knife that Pop gave me. One day I was trying to split a wooden spool. I don't have any idea why. Really smart. I put the spool against my stomach, stuck the point of the knife into the hole, and pulled the knife toward me. The spool split and the knife went straight into my stomach.

I never reported it. I thought they'd take the knife away from me. It finally healed, but I've still got the scar.

You could have killed yourself!

John used to climb around up in the cupolas in the top of the new barn. He used to climb up to the harpoon track—the hay fork track up there—and go hand over hand down the track from one cupola to another. There were three up there. Oh, man, that was high. It was a terrible drop down to the barn floor. And you know, I couldn't look at him. Hand over hand. It scared me to death to see him climbing around up there. He had to prove to himself that he could do it, and he had to prove it to everybody else, too. I think he was the only guy that ever went into all three of those cupolas.

I was.

They did their own butchering out there—pigs and beef cattle. I don't remember getting much of either to eat, but they made what was called "crackling" from the pigs. Now, they call it "scrapple." They stored it up in the top of the chicken house, and boy, was it good! We used to sneak up there and get as much as we could.

There was even a little meat in it once in a while, whenever they killed a big-enough hog.

Larry was up there stealing some one day, and somebody hollered to him that somebody was coming. He tried to jump onto the ladder and climb down, but he missed and fell and broke his wrist.

Fell right out of the window!

I remember him coming into the Home, and his arm came over like this, down like this, and out like that.

Compound fracture of the wrist. I broke it four times out there, and one time they had to re-break it and reset it because it had been set crooked.

Doc Schumaker and Uncle Elmer did the job. And all the kids were on the fire escape, looking through the windows and watching what was going on.

They gave me ether, but they didn't give me enough, because I could feel them trying to re-break it. While I was out, while they were working on it, one of them noticed that my face had turned blue. Uncle Elmer finally looked in my mouth and discovered that I had swallowed my tongue. I never had much use for him, but he saved my life that time.

Of course, Larry didn't have to go out and work on the farm while his wrist was healing, but they made him work inside

with his one good arm. One day he had to paint a table in the living room. I remember he painted it yellow.

Some of the kids came in at noon that day, after Miss Frank had gone to lunch. Skunk Perry walked in and Larry said to him, "Hey Skunk, look at the great job I did painting this table!"

Skunk said, "You didn't paint that. You're a liar."

That burned Larry up, so he took a swing at Skunk. Of course Larry's arm was still in a cast and a sling, so he only had one hand to use, and Skunk was beating up on him.

Just then, John came in and saw what was going on.

I came in and saw that and went crazy. I got ahold of Skunk and threw him down and was beating the hell out of him—pounding his head on the floor—when Miss Frank came in. I was so berserk I didn't even know she was there. She tried to pull me off, but she couldn't. So she picked up a tennis racket and hit me behind the ear with it. She laid the top of my head open, too, and it knocked me out.

Somebody carried me in and put me on a cot in her little sewing room. When I came to, she was standing there with the racket still in her hand. I was so scared that I jumped up and ran out into the yard and wouldn't come in. When it was almost time to go to bed, she came out and finally coaxed me in.

Regina Frank was one of the nicest people there. Really the kindest of all the matrons I had, but I still have the lump she gave me behind my ear.

One day I developed a boil on my left shin, but it didn't heal. So I was taken to a doctor's office in Bellevue and had it lanced. For some reason it still didn't heal, so Miss Frank sent Skunk Perry out to the barnyard to get a cup of cow manure. She told him to be sure it was fresh, and when he brought it back she made a poultice of it and put it on the boil. I don't know why, but it did bring the boil to a head and eventually cured it.

The orphanage was a strict religious home. The church was less than a quarter of a mile away.

So we used to walk down, two-by-two.

On Sundays, it was Sunday school, then a two-hour service with a sermon spoken in German. When Reverend Wengard was transferred, the next pastor gave the sermons in English. On Sunday evenings, it was YPA—Young People's Alliance—and then another sermon. Midweek, it was prayer meeting. We had to go to all of them. And we had to sing hymns and read the Bible after every meal and take a course in Evangelical catechism.

To this day I can recall the first question in the catechism: "What is the chief end of man?" Answer: "The chief end of man is to glorify God and enjoy Him forever."

We had to go to church all the time out there. That's why we got so sick of church that we don't go anymore.

Left to Right:
Clara Diehl, June Beidelman,
Ilerda Eckert, Clara Christ, Tessie
DiDio, Mantana Eckert. Ebenezer Orphan Home,
Flat Rock, Ohio. c. 1912.
(Eckert-Sauerwine family archive)

One time in church—I don't know if you remember—I fell in love with this girl. I said to John, "John, you go over there and tell her that I'm in love with her."

So he went over and told her, and she said, "Tell him that I'm in love with him, too."

That was the last time I ever saw her.

Remember when Tessie DiDio came out there? A little Italian girl. She came after we had been there for a while. She had rosy cheeks and curly hair. She was like a little doll. Everybody loved her.

I fell in love with all the new girls who came there, you know. They were all pretty girls and I fell in love very easily.

Social contact with the girls was almost nil. Of course, we saw them in school and church and around the Home. But the only time we were really allowed to play games and socialize with them was at the annual Fourth of July picnic on the front lawn. And, of course, that was under strict supervision.

One time, though, I got lucky. Some of the girls were making braided rugs up in the attic, and I was told to go up there and help them sew carpet rags. They were all so pretty! It was like going to a prayer meeting without any prayers.

One of Uncle Elmer's responsibilities was to teach physical education, so he set up a girls' basketball program. One day he said, "Now, tonight, the girls are going to play basketball out in the barn, and I don't want to see any boys out there." Well, hell! Those girls wore bloomers down to their ankles, almost!

Of course, when he and the girls showed up, a big gang of boys was hiding up in the haymows on both sides of the stairway. When the girls started playing basketball, Oscar Spangaro was watching them through a knothole at the top of the steps. Somebody came up behind him and pushed him, and he fell all the way down the stairway and out onto the barn floor. Well, kids ran all over everywhere, and Uncle Elmer took off after Oscar.

I ran out to the barnyard and stood under the barn overhang for a while, so I didn't get caught.

A bunch of kids ran home and jumped in bed. Pretty soon, Uncle Elmer came into the bedroom. He stopped at every bed, and every once in a while he would say to some kid, "Get out in the middle of the floor." He got five or six kids out there—everybody who was breathing hard—and he gave every one of them a licking with the strap. He had a real sadistic streak in him.

One day Uncle Elmer saw a sparrow hawk flying over the field. It landed in a tree at the edge of the woods, and he picked up a .22 and shot it. It fell like a lead weight down out of the tree, and I felt terrible about that. I couldn't understand why he did it. He was an avid bird-watcher, you know, and eventually he became quite prominent in the Audobon Society.

A feral cat came onto orphanage property one day and killed a chicken. They caught it and tied it to a wagon wheel with a string, and Uncle Elmer shot that, too.

William Beck was a hard-working guy, and a pretty good-sized kid. He wasn't a troublemaker. He was quiet and unassuming. But he did something wrong one day, and Uncle Elmer said, "I want to see you in the classroom after school." So William walked into the room after school, and Uncle Elmer took off his belt. William reached into his back pocket and pulled out a knife. Then he said, "You hit me once with that strap, and I'll cut you to pieces."

Uncle Elmer folded his belt, turned around, and walked out of the room. He was so afraid of Beck that he didn't dare report him. And he didn't touch any of the other bigger guys after that, either. Those guys were tough.

Remember Pop Zerman?

Pop Zerman and his sons, Bert and Zim Zerman. He was the farm manager. He and his family lived in the little house by the old barn. He didn't have much hired help, but he didn't need much. The kids did most of the work.

I think he had three paid helpers. One of them was Stiffy McClure. He was young, and a real nice guy.

He came in one night after supper and said, "Anybody around here got a broom?" and I said, "Yes," and went and got him one. Then he said, "Now, I'm going to make this broom stand up all by itself." So he sat down and spit on the end of it—you know, on the handle end—and stood it up like this in front of him. Then all of a sudden he let go of it, and the broom stood there all by itself. I couldn't believe it! I thought it was real magic!

He always did that trick in a dark corner. Come to find out, he had a long black thread stitched between his knees. When he sat down, he'd just spread his knees to tighten the thread and then lean the broom against it. Nobody could see the thread.

When I finally found out it wasn't magic, I was so disappointed! I wasted hours trying to stand that broom up on end like that!

Fritz Weber used to have a .22 rifle that they butchered with. I remember they took the bull out to the old barn one day and tied him between two posts. Then Weber stood back with the .22 and shot him between the eyes. The bull just stood there and shook his head. Just stood there. They finally hit him in the head with a sledge, and he went down.

They killed him with a sledgehammer. That wasn't a very appetizing sight.

Out there they had what they called a cloak closet where you'd hang your barn clothes when you came in off the farm. If you had overalls on, you'd take them off and hang them up in there. We kept our work shoes in there, too.

One night somebody said to me, "Hey, Skunk wants to see you in the cloak room." So I went in, and it was pitch dark in there. Somebody slammed the door behind me, and all of a sudden shoes flew at me from all over the place. When they finally let me out, they made me go tell somebody else, "Hey, Skunk wants to see you in the cloak room," and they'd go in there and, "Whoom! Bang!"

An August 17, 1913 outing at Cedar Point Park on Lake Erie near Sandusky, Ohio. Laurence Buchholz is third from the left, front row; Gerald Beck is the first boy on the right, top row. The lady in the center of the top row may be matron Regina Frank.
(Buchholz family archive)

One of our dirty tricks was to find a nest of rotten eggs and then slip up behind somebody. Our overalls were always too big—baggy, you know—and you'd drop an egg in his pocket and then say, "Gee, you're a good scout!" and slap him in the pocket and keep on going.

There was a kid out there named Henry Fluege who could pick a bumblebee off a flower and hold it in his hand, and it never stung him.

Some of the kids used to catch bumblebees by the wings, you know, and they'd sneak up behind somebody and hold the bee against his ankle and watch him holler and hop around when the bee stung him. Boy, was that fun!

Bumblebees used to make their nests in the ground along the fence row. We used to stand out in the field and look for a bumblebee on a blossom and then follow it back to the nest.

We made paddles out of wooden shingles. We'd draw straws to see who had to hit the nest to get the bees out. Then, everybody who wanted honey would dig like crazy and swat the bees with their paddles. We usually got stung, but it was worth it. There was honey in some of the pods, but there were grubs in others. They were all the same size, so you never knew which you were eating. We didn't care. They were both good.

I saw Gerald Beck come back from one of those once. He was almost unrecognizable. His upper lip was hanging down over his chin. His face was all distorted and he could hardly see out of his good eye. He was blind in the other eye. I don't know how that happened.

They used to store big barrels of sauerkraut down in the basement where they separated the milk. Nobody was allowed in the basement, but it was underneath the Home, so you could sneak down there.

One day we were playing a game called "Fox and Geese." The geese would start by laying down a stick pointing in the direction they were going. After a while, the foxes would start out after them and try to find them.

Larry and I and some other kids were the geese. We went down around the orchard, around the barn and then back to the Home. We ran down into the cellar and hid behind some barrels of sauerkraut. There must have been a dozen of them down there.

When the foxes came in looking for us, we could see them silhouetted against the outside door opening. So everybody picked up big handfuls of sauerkraut and heaved it at them.

Then the foxes threw it back at us, and we threw it back at them.

Well, eventually there was sauerkraut all over that basement and all over everybody!

Somebody heard us down there.

Miss Frank came down and said, "Everybody upstairs," and we had to go up and sit down and wait. Pretty soon, Father and Mother Messerschmidt came in, and Mother Messerschmidt said, "I want everybody who was down in that basement to come out here and stand in the middle of the floor."

Nobody went. So she walked around the room and smelled everybody's hands. When she got to me, I said, "I was only walking past outside when the sauerkraut came sailing up out of there and hit me. I was just brushing it off."

"Well, then," she said, "you get a licking for being where you shouldn't have been."

John saw her coming and took out a piece of peppermint candy and rubbed his hands with it. And she couldn't smell the sauerkraut when she got to him!

So I got a licking that night. Oh, boy, what a flock of kids got a licking with the strap that night. But John didn't get it because of his peppermint candy.

They never baled hay out there. It was all pitched, and we had to mow it away in the mow, too. They had a harpoon, and they'd pull the hay up and drop it any old place and the kids had to mow it away.

We used to get up on the rafters there and somersault maybe twenty or thirty feet into the hay. Dive, you know, and flip over.

There were these slatted windows in the barn to let air in. There was one in the back of the barn, and we had little rooms in the hay back there with tunnels leading into them. But they didn't know we had tunnels in there, and to get out of work we used to get in there, and nobody could find us.

One Sunday afternoon we were running around in the barn and somebody saw Father Messerschmidt coming, and everybody crawled into the tunnels. I can remember him standing down there on the barn floor hollering at the kids, but nobody moved a muscle.

Everybody waited till he left, and then we came out of there like fleas off a dog.

I remember another Sunday afternoon we were playing Fox and Geese, and the geese hid up in the hayloft where the beams went across. The hay was piled on top of the poles and under the beams, you know. We were out there playing, and all of a sudden somebody came up the stairs and hollered, "Hey!

Father Messerschmidt's coming!" Some of us got away before he got there, but the rest went up into the hay mow.

Father Messerschmidt started looking for everybody at the bottom of the mow. Just as he was going to crawl into one of those tunnels, some kid accidentally slid off the mow and landed right on top of him and beat it out of there.

There was a Christmas tree in the dining room every year. We sang Christmas carols and we hung stockings on our boxes in the living room. They'd usually put an orange and some Brazil nuts and a little bag of candy—Christmas candy—in them. Once in a while they'd give us a small toy. One year I got a harmonica that I taught myself to play, but I don't remember who gave it to me.

Christmas out there wasn't much. Sometimes we'd get new overalls or a pair of shoes. I don't recall any toys at all. I always wished for a pair of roller skates, but, of course, I never got them.

Pop sent us each a pair of ice skates one Christmas, though. Clamp skates. They were too big for our shoes, so we had to make wooden pegs and put them along the side of our soles and then clamp the skates on.

Water would lay in low spots out in the fields, so we'd find one of those that had frozen over to skate on. But usually there was a lot of stubble poking up through the ice, and the skates wouldn't stay on our shoes anyway, so down we'd go!

You know, we made our own sleds out there. We'd get a couple of barrel staves—they were bow-shaped, like this—and use them for the runners. Then we'd nail a wooden box—or whatever wood we could find—between them so we'd have something to sit on. And we put ropes through the staves so we could drag the sled back up the hill out at the barn. You couldn't steer those things. They went sideways and any old way they wanted to!

We made our own kites, too, out of sticks and newspaper. I don't remember where we got those newspapers.

I earned a box kite once. It was a beauty! I sent away for a case of White Cloverine salve, and I sold it for a quarter a can to the people that worked at the orphanage. The matrons, the teachers, anybody I could get to buy it.

I remember they sent you some religious pictures with the salve.

Every time you sold a can, you gave away a free religious picture with it. And most of the people out there wanted the picture more than they wanted the salve.

When I sold it all, I sent the money to the White Cloverine Salve Company in Tyrone, Pennsylvania. I remember that! Tyrone, Pennsylvania!

Then I waited for my kite. I thought it would never come, but finally it did.

Later, I sold another case and got a set of those circular propellers that you push up off a spiral steel shaft. Those things would sail thirty or forty feet in the air! Just like a helicopter!

We made a bicycle out there. Actually, it wasn't much of a bicycle. We found an old frame someplace. There weren't any handlebars on it, so we stuck a piece of broomstick through the hole. We found two iron wheelbarrow wheels and put them on it.

We couldn't pedal it, because it didn't have any pedals. But at least we could ride it downhill.

We pushed it up to the top of the barn hill and coasted all the way down. There was no seat, so we sat on the frame. It was a pretty rough ride!

They had a baseball diamond out there at one time, out in back of the back yard, out where they used to keep the sheep. We never had a baseball, but we'd tie rags up with string. You know—we'd wrap the string around and around...

...and then, if we could find some tape, we'd tape it. We'd hit it with a stick. A piece of broomstick. But usually the first guy that hit it would knock the tape off.

Larry, Doris and John Buchholz. This photo was taken during Wm. C. and Doris Buchholz's 1914 visit to the Orphan Home. Doris: "Miss Frank combed my hair and fixed me up to go down and have our picture taken."
(Buchholz family archive)

≈

It was about 1914 when Pop came out to see us again, and he brought our sister, Doris, with him. Boy, she was a good-looking girl.

I didn't know her. I didn't remember her. She was a stranger to me. They both seemed like strangers to me by that time. She would have been about eight years old then. We had our picture taken in Bellevue. Doris had a ribbon in her hair. Larry was on the left in the picture, Doris was in the middle, and I was on the right.

Powerful-looking guys we were, too, weren't we?

≈

When you got older and went out to the barn to be a barn boy, you became a man.

Each barn boy had three cows to milk and feed. John and I had to take care of them for one week, then two other guys would take care of them for the next week. It was just like having your own cows. We had to go out with them— take them out to pasture—and go get them in the morning and bring them home.

At one time, all the cows were named after the Greek

alphabet, but as the herd grew to forty or fifty, they had to give the new ones other names. My three were Alpha, Gamma and Alma. I took care of them for four years or more. John had Blackie, Rosie and another one after one of his died.

We had to milk them, dung them out and keep them brushed down. We had to weigh the milk and record the weight, then pour it into a separating tank and turn it by hand to separate the cream from the milk.

Whenever it was decided to make butter, quite a few days before they started the operation all the milk had to be taken to the house and run through the DeLaval cream separator. I can still picture the basement where it was located.

The first time I took my milk to be separated, I saw all that nice cream coming out of the spout and I thought, "Oh, boy, now's my chance to get my fill!" It looked delicious. But I made a hog of myself and got sick as a dog. That was the last time I tried that.

It used to be sort of a game among us to see who could get their barn work done first. The barn lights were controlled from the powerhouse, where the electricity was generated, and the powerhouse engineer always turned the lights on about sunup.

One morning I decided to be the first guy done with his chores. I managed to wake up before anyone else and got my milk pail and went out to the barn. When I got there, I found that the lights hadn't been turned on yet, although dawn was just breaking. But I went down to where the cows were stanchioned with my milk pail on my arm.

Just as I turned in the gate to get to my cows, the first one in line gave a big cough and let loose with a shot of watery dung. It caught me on my right shoulder and hit my milk pail, so I had to go back to the big house and put on a new set of clothes and clean my milk pail and go back and do my chores.

I was kidded about that for weeks.

Once in a great while, the girls didn't get our milk pails out at night for the morning milking. On those occasions, we had to go into the kitchen for the pails, and on the way in we passed a big drawer where they threw all the old bread that they used for our bread and milk. I used to sneak a handful of that bread when I went by the drawer and take it out to the barn. As I milked, I'd squirt a stream of nice, fresh, warm milk on it and eat it.

Now, people think that cows are dumb, but they knew me. I could go out to the field where they were grazing and call them, and they would come right over to the fence. And I milked those cows I guess for four years or more, just like they were my own. And when it was my turn to feed them, they got more than any other cow. Every once in a while an extra pail of ensilage would go into those cows. When there was any salt around, they got salt. It was just like you owned them.

And one of them had a calf—a bull calf. I had so much fun with him! He could run! Oh, how he could run and gambol! Somehow I heard about Dan Patch, the racehorse, so that's what I called him. I weaned him myself. I'd stick my finger in his mouth and then pull his head down into the milk bucket. He was just like my own little calf.

Then one day I went out to the barn, and somebody told me they had taken him to the butcher. I couldn't believe anybody could do such a thing. I tell you, it almost broke my heart.

You know, it's a wonder that some of the kids didn't get gored to death. Oh, boy, they had some mean bulls out there, and they always had to put rings in their noses. Then they had a long pole with a snap on the end so they could lead the bull out to the watering trough and back.

Remember there was blood in the ground where they butchered? And the bull would smell that blood and paw in that stuff and kick the dirt as high as the barn with his front hooves. He was a big one. If he had ever got loose he would have made some trouble.

They had some sheep out there, and they had a ram. And that ram was something! One day the sheep were grazing in the peach orchard, and John and I went into the orchard to get some peaches. Well, when the ram saw us, he took off after us, and up a tree we went!

Do you think that he'd let us down? Oh, no! He'd be grazing around down there and John would say, "Now's a good time to sneak down." So we'd climb down, almost get to the ground, and the ram was up and away he'd come! We'd have been there all night if somebody hadn't finally come and coaxed him away from us.

Remember when some new kids would come, or somebody did you something wrong and you wanted to get even with them? We managed to catch the ram and take him out to the field and hold him by the horns. Then we'd bring the kid out and start him toward the fence, and the minute the kid started to run, the ram would take off after him. If the kid didn't get to the fence on time, the ram would knock him down.

We didn't have anything to play with out there, so we had to make our own fun. And that was fun!

The most fun, though, was stomping ensilage.

Silage—chopped-up field corn; ears, stalks, and leaves—that we would pack into the silo and feed to the cows in the winter. They would shoot it up to the top of the silo through a long pipe and it would come blowing down inside. The guy handling the chute inside would have to see that it was evenly distributed and tamped down, so he'd chase the kids around the inside of the silo with the blower. He'd point it at you, and the ensilage would sting whenever it hit you on the legs, so you'd have to keep running and tamping it down.

Tell them about Fritz Weber and William Diehl.

Fritz Weber was a big, husky Deutschman. I saw him take two twenty-five pound bags of flour, pick them up, and hold them out straight, like this. Fifty pounds.

He was a powerful guy. Fritz Weber.

When he came to work at the orphanage, he brought his son, Fred, with him. Fred was sort of a pet, because his father worked there. One day when we were working up in the silo he was in there watching us. He stayed up at the top of the ladder so he could be the first one out. When it came time for us to climb down, William Diehl followed Fred down the ladder and accidentally stepped on his fingers.

Fred went over to where his father was standing on the wagon—on the corn rigging, feeding the corn—and told him about it. Then Fritz called William over to the wagon and reached down and picked him up—by his head—onto the wagon.

Then he hit him and snapped him in the back of the neck. William jumped off the wagon and ran over to the silo and beat his head against it, trying to kill himself. He banged his head all up, and it drove him nuts for a while.

It must have been terrible. Fritz Weber was a big, powerful German, that guy. He had muscles that stood out like a blacksmith's.

Years later, Bob Morris told us that William Diehl was killed a short time after we left the orphanage.

He was playing out in the shed where they stored the coal and firewood. A shaft ran out of the boiler house and into the shed. The shaft had a wheel on the end and a belt ran from it and powered the saw they used to cut up logs. William was up there, and somehow he backed into the shaft.

He got caught up—tangled up—in the shaft.

It caught his clothes and rolled them up, and it kept spinning him around and around and slamming...he got all smashed up, all broken up. That was terrible. That was bad.

How did the threshing operation work there at the farm? We put all the wheat up in the barn. When they could get the threshing machine to come around—and the steam roller—they would park it between the hay mows, with the wheat on each side. And we would get up there in the mow and throw it down onto the moving belt that took it to the thresher. Then there was a big pipe that went out and moved the straw up to the top of the stack out in the barnyard.

The tractor was outside, just where the hill went up

to the barn—the upper level of the barn. There the tractor stood, just at the top of the hill.

The belt...

...a big, long belt...

...came in, hooked onto the thresher, and went outside. They fired it with coal and wood.

But boy, the job was out on the stacks. Barley, bringing the stack up. They'd keep you out there, and you'd have to keep the stack square, you know. Then they'd turn the blower on you to keep you moving. And all the awns, you know—the beards...

...down your neck.

They were terrible.

Boy, I used to hate that threshing. I thought that was terrible. But they used to come around with buckets of cherryade, remember that?

Yeah. Cherry or berry, either one.

That's the only time you got it, when you were working out there.

Big dipper in a pail. Talk about nectar of the gods. That was it.

Pretty color, and tasted…oh boy, did that taste good! It was a contractor who had the thresher.

They would hire a guy to come in.

And they would go for shares, or work it out somehow.

As we used up the straw and eventually got down to the bottom of the pile, the rats would run out of there. Man, were they big, weren't they? Big rats. And we tried to scare them with the pitchforks, and they'd stand right up on their hind legs. They were living in that straw pile, you know. Talk about a hotel. They had it made!

One day some of us were working over in the Eighty, and the foreman left us there alone. We wandered over onto Goode's farm, and down the field a little way we found a hole in the ground that we could crawl into. We didn't know what it was, so we didn't dare crawl in too far, but once we got in there, it looked like a large cave.

Fred Fadley had sent away for a carbide light, so a couple days later we borrowed it from him and went back. We took a ball of string with us and tied it to a rock. Then we crawled in and explored until we came to the end of the string. It was a huge cavern with several levels descending into the ground.

I'm sure we didn't discover it, but I think we may have been the first ones from the orphanage to go into it. Today, it's called "Seneca Caverns," and we've heard that it's quite a tourist attraction.

The time that John and I discovered the cupola on the wagon shed, that was the time!

The wagon shed had a nice little cupola on it.

It was about four feet square.

And I found a way to get up there.

It had little ridges around it that were open to let air out.

I found a way to get up to it without a ladder, so nobody else would know how to get up there. It was where the struts came up…

…and the shingles were nailed on.

You could get your fingers in there between the boards and your toes against the bottom, and you could work your way up to it and get up in there. Well, when Larry found that out, the two of us used to get up there, and we made a regular little cozy nest out of it.

We got up there, and we hauled boards up and made a floor. We went over to the railroad and stole a switch lamp— a little kerosene switch lamp about three inches square with a little chimney on it—and put that up there. We got pieces of glass and laid them up against the windows to keep the cold air from drifting through. We had window shades so the light wouldn't shine out at night. We got apples and put them up there. We had a board between us, stretching across so we could put the lantern on it. John used to play on one side and I on the other. And we had the apples and everything. Then we decided to put another floor underneath that one. Remember? We had a double floor so if anybody came in they couldn't see us. It was a makeshift affair, but we had our private room up there, and nobody knew it except John and me. Nobody ever attempted to go up there. It was a tough climb, and dangerous. When we got up there, we used to stay awhile, and when the days were real dark, we would light that switch lamp. Oh, we used to sit in our own little room, you know, eating our apples.

But we didn't tell anybody about it. Oh, ho, no siree. That was our little private spot. We had it boarded up so you couldn't see up in there. We had it made.

Then, one day in the fall of 1916, when I was almost fifteen, we were told that Father Messerschmidt wanted to see us. We didn't know what to expect. We went to his office and sat, and he finally came in and told us that our family had sent for us and that we were going home.

It was the most wonderful day of my life.

They didn't keep children there after they were sixteen. I was only thirteen, but, fortunately, I think the family knew that Larry and I were close, and they didn't want to leave me there alone.

We were close. There were no brothers out there who were any closer than we were.

I don't think those six years did us any real harm. We learned to work out in the fields like full-fledged men—pitching hay, cutting sugar beets, feeding livestock, cutting corn, stomping ensilage and digging potatoes. And we had some good times.

The day before we left for home, they gave us the day off. We didn't have to work, and they gave us permission to go up in the belfry. We went up and looked out over the farm and identified all the fields: the Thirteen, the Seventeen, the Fifteen...

...and the Twenty-one, the Thirty-one, and the Twenty-eight...

…and the Thirty-five! And we looked out over the Thirteen and could see the houses in Flat Rock.

A bird's eye view.

That's one of the experiences that has stuck in my memory ever since.

I don't remember much about the ride back to Geneva.

We went home by train. We went alone.

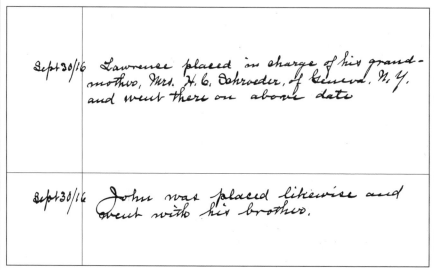

1916 Orphan Home Journal Entry
(Flat Rock Home archive)

*W*E GOT TO GENEVA ON SUNDAY MORNING, *October first. I don't remember who met us at the Lehigh Valley station, but they took us down to Grandma Schroeder's house at 185 North Main Street right away.*

We walked in there, and we didn't know anybody. They called our brother Lester down from upstairs when we came in, and that's the first time I realized I had a kid brother. I had never thought about it. I just barely remembered him being held in my mother's arms.

Lester Buchholz c. 1912
(Buchholz family archive)

He was too shy to come down and say hello, so he just sat on the steps.

In 1929, when Lester and I were on our way back to Geneva from California, we stopped at the Orphan Home. And you know, when we pulled in the driveway out there, across the lawn came an elderly, gray-haired lady.

I recognized her and got out of the car and walked over toward her. I said, "Miss Frank," and she said, "John Buchholz."

It was Regina Frank. It had been thirteen years—from 1916 to 1929—and I was surprised that she recognized me.

Then she looked over toward the car and said, "Where is Laurence?"

Regina Frank was probably the best one of them all out there.

Yeah, but she's the one who beat me up.

I know, but that was only an isolated incident.

We went back in 1966 for the 100th anniversary celebration, and thirteen or fourteen were there that we knew. Blanche Froom, Robert Froom, Clarence Hunsinger and Otto DiDio were there. Skunk Perry came up to us. He was the mayor of a town down in Delaware. We saw Tessie DiDio, the pretty Italian girl that everyone was in love with. We saw Bob Morris. He lives in Pennsylvania near the Delaware Water Gap. We still correspond with him and stop in to visit him sometimes.

Corrine Hellinger was there, and we used to write to her, but she passed away. Cornelia Wriver was there, too. We still write to her.

Saw Stiffy McClure. And Grace and Ilerda Eckert and Emma Fowler.

It was so good to get out there, but there were changes, disappointments, and changes in perspective. Distances had changed.

We used to think that from the house to the barn was a long way. You could hit it with a rock today. Do you remember how far it used to seem from the barn to the house when you were carrying a pail of milk? I swear if anybody had told me when I was a kid that I'd be able to throw a stone that far, I wouldn't have believed them.

The orchard was gone. The woods had changed. Remember there were big woods and little woods, and in between was that bunch of young growth? That was all changed.

We looked for our initials up in the belfry, but they'd been covered with aluminum. The swimming hole was still there, but we didn't get a chance to go down there.

I'm sorry we didn't.

But I remember seeing it as we walked across the road.

I'd expected to see the big barn where I'd spent so much time, but it was gone. That was a disappointment. It had burned down in 1966.

Before we got there.

And the wagon shed had burned down, too. We wondered if maybe some kids had found our old switch lamp up in the cupola and lit it and knocked it over and burned the place down.
It had been fifty years since we had been back there together. 1916 to 1966.

$\mathcal{I}$N 1917, SHORTLY AFTER HIS RETURN TO GENEVA, Larry found work as a printer's apprentice at The Geneva Daily Times. Later that year, he delivered grocery orders by horse-drawn wagon throughout the city for his Uncle Arthur Schroeder's company, Merchants' Delivery Service.

Larry was hired by the Lehigh Valley Railroad as a signal gang laborer working out of Geneva in 1918, and that year nearly succumbed to a long, delirious bout with influenza.

During a brief layoff from the railroad in 1919, he was employed by the U.S. Radiator Works, and that same year he took John, then 16, into Dan Deegan's Saloon on Exchange Street and bought him his first beer. ("It tasted so bad I couldn't drink it," John remembered. "But four or five years later, beer didn't taste so bad after all.")

Later in 1919, at the encouragement of his older brother, Bill, Larry left Geneva for Lyndhurst, New Jersey, where he worked as a hostler and fireman for the Delaware, Lackawanna and Western Railroad in its Kingsland Shops. But a 1920 strike left him unemployed, and the urge to fly led him to join the Army Air Force. In February, 1921, Larry was certified as "physically fit for flying" and appointed as a 5th Aerosquadron Cadet at Mitchell Field, Long Island, New York. As a pilot, he also flew out of Kelly Field, San Antonio, Texas; Carlstrom Field, Arcadia, Florida; and Langley Field, Virginia, before he was injured in a crash-landing on a beach at Rockport, Maine.

Upon discharge in 1924, Larry returned to the Delaware, Lackawanna and Western, working first as a railroad detective and later as a stationary fireman.

A layoff left him again unemployed, but in 1925 he found a job delivering flowers for an East Orange florist, and it was there that he discovered a flair for and love of arranging that led to a 42-year career as a florist in East Orange and Bloomfield.

During the late 1920s, he became a licensed amateur radio operator, building his own short-wave transmitter and receiver. A few years later, he taught himself to play the electric Hawaiian steel guitar.

Larry married Marion Smith, a registered nurse, in Manhattan's Little Church Around the Corner in 1931, and they lived happily and comfortably together in Nutley, New Jersey, through his 1968 retirement and until her sudden passing in 1972. After Marion's death, Larry continued his duties as a school crossing guard at a nearby corner in Nutley, dispensing wisdom, humor and bubblegum to his little charges.

At age eighty-five, still drinking a nightly Manhattan, he bought and learned to play a Hammond organ. Three of his favorite songs were *Drifting and Dreaming, Blue Hawaii* and *My Isle of Golden Dreams*.

Larry was a charming, gregarious, charismatic, good man who loved life. When he entered a room, it lit up.

On November 23, 1992—his ninety-first birthday—he wrote, "I made it!" on his calendar. Five days later, congestive heart failure claimed him.

He is buried in Glendale Cemetery, Bloomfield, NJ.

After returning to Geneva from the orphanage, John entered eighth grade at the Lewis Street School. He and Larry lived with their widowed step-grandmother, Margaret Schroeder, for whom John stoked the furnace, carried out ashes, mowed the lawn, shoveled snow, and played hymns on the mandolin.

"She was a kindly old lady," he remembered years later, "but at the time, I didn't appreciate that, because she continued the discipline I had had at the Orphan Home. We had prayers at mealtime and went to church three times on Sunday and prayer meeting every Wednesday night."

John worked after school at the Smith & Long grocery store on Castle Street for a time, then at the Harry Rigby and A&P grocery stores. Other boyhood employers included Rice's Nursery, Geneva Auto Company, the Charles Holliday farm, Merchants' Delivery Service, Easy Washer Sales, Geneva Preserving Works, Nagel & Trickler Construction, the U.S. Lens Company, and a host of others in and around Geneva.

In 1922, after his graduation from Geneva High School, John found employment with the Lehigh Valley Railroad as an assistant signal maintainer, working out of Geneva. That job led to decade-long service as a lineman and line foreman for Lehigh Valley and Pacific Bell of California, with cherished relationships and colorful, rough-and-tumble experiences he would document in his written memories some seventy years later. In 1999, his award-winning reminiscence, *Lehigh Days: Memories of a Railroad Lineman*, was published posthumously in *Crown Jewels* magazine.

Following his employment as a lineman, John served for seventeen years as club manager and secretary of the 1,500-member Waverly, NY, Moose Lodge. During that time he married Agnes Barrows, whose ill-health resulted in their 1950 move to the arid climate of Arizona and New Mexico. There, during a two-year stay, John was at various times a fire-alarm installer, tungsten mill manager, quarter-horse owner, independent cattle buyer, and oil well speculator.

Back East in 1953, they bought "The Little Store" in Dundee, New York, and he and Agnes successfully ran that small-town retail grocery business until 1957, when Agnes's health required another move, this time to Florida, where they found work managing "Twin Towers," an apartment complex in Hollywood Beach.

But their faltering marital relationship resulted in a return North in 1960. That year, upon the collapse of his marriage, John moved into his sister's cottage on the Susquehanna River near Barton, New York. He managed a retail appliance store in Waverly until his retirement in the 1970s.

John remained physically active during retirement, and one of his great pleasures was hiking a nearby abandoned roadbed of the Lehigh Valley Railroad along the Susquehanna, recovering cross-arm insulators that he might well have wired as a young lineman decades before.

"I was a jack-of-all-trades, master of none," he once wrote, but strangers who sat at a poker table with him or challenged him to a game of straight pool quickly found out otherwise. And those who knew him well also differed with his view. He was a successful businessman, astute investor, and a logical, lightning-fast thinker. He was also a loyal friend and honest, generous and loving man.

In his 1993, 32,000-word autobiography, he wrote, "Here are a few of my life's most vivid memories: seeing Halley's Comet in 1910; arriving at The Ebenezer Orphan Home later that same year; learning of my mother's death in 1911 and realizing that I would never get to know her; witnessing the grandeur of the Grand Canyon in 1928; discovering, at our first reunion in 1926, that I had a real family; and, in 1992, learning that I had lost my brother Larry and was the sole survivor of that family."

John died of renal failure in Paoli, Pennsylvania, on July 20, 1994. His ashes are buried in a small rural cemetery in Lockwood, New York, along a former route of the Lehigh Valley Railroad.

In 1926, Larry, John, Bill, Doris, Lester and their father gathered on the north shore of Seneca Lake in Geneva for what would be the first of sixty-four consecutive family reunions, usually week-long and held in upstate New York's Finger Lakes region.

As they parted each year, the brothers—who called each other "Luke"—sang *God Be with You Till We Meet Again* in harmony that would move your soul.

John H. & Larry K. Buchholz c. 1986.
(John A. Buchholz)

* *photograph*

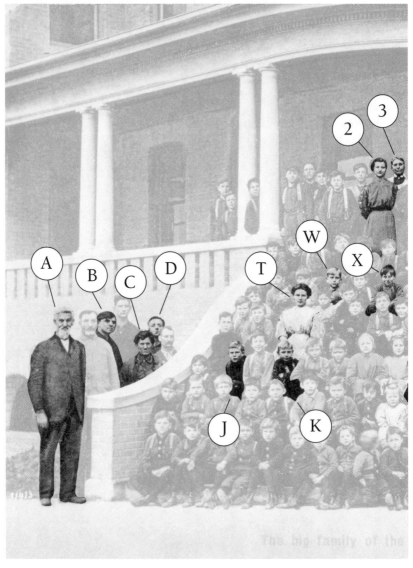

A–Rev. William H. Messerschmidt
B–Cooper (power house worker)
C–Pop Zerman (farm manager)
D–Julius Zimmerman ("Mikie Dobber")
E–Clara Christ
F–Grace Eckert
G–Tessie DiDio
H–Dooty (matron)

I–Wetzel (matron)
J–John H. Buchholz
K–John Schrader? Robert Morris?
L–Mantana Eckert
M–Emma Seitz
N–Caroline Messerschmidt
O–Clara Diehl
P–Ilerda Eckert

Ebenezer Orphan Home

Q–June Beidelman
R–Maggie Pfeiffer Hammer? (guest)
S–Messerschmidt (orphanmother)
T–Haegle? (matron)
U–Cora Morris?
V–Lily Sydow? (teacher)
W–Lawrence Schrader
X–Arthur Eckert

Y–Laurence K. Buchholz
Z–Lena Schroeder Schmalzried (teacher)
1–Sofia Frank (matron)
2–Knaus? (teacher)
3–Regina Frank (matron)
4–Kelty (child, cook's daughter)
5–Kelty (cook)